7th grad.

MILLCREEK — WEST UNITY SCHOOL
WEST UNITY OHIO

796.332
Aas
c.1

Aaseng, Nathan
College football: You are the coach

DATE DUE			
12/5/86 B.W.			
OCT. 23 1987			
DEC. 01 1987			
DEC. 17 1987			
NOV 22 1988			
MAR 03 1989			
MAY 10 1989			
SEP 14 1989			
JAN 24 1991			
DEC 17 1991			
C.L. 10/12			

116   85

MEDIALOG
Alexandria, Ky 41001

COLLEGE FOOTBALL: YOU are the COACH

Nate Aaseng

 Lerner Publications Company ▪ Minneapolis

To Doug Kunkle
and other incurable
college sports fans

Copyright © 1984 by Lerner Publications Company

All rights reserved. International copyright secured. No part of this book may be reproduced in any form whatsoever without permission in writing from the publisher except for the inclusion of brief quotations in an acknowledged review.

Manufactured in the United States of America

LIBRARY OF CONGRESS CATALOGING IN PUBLICATION DATA

Aaseng, Nathan.
College football—you are the coach.

Summary: The reader is invited to make coaching decisions at crucial moments in ten college bowl games. Provides the actual decisions and their outcomes.
    1. Football—Coaching—Juvenile literature.
2. Football—United States—Juvenile literature.
3. College sports—United States—Juvenile literature.
[1. Football—Coaching] I. Title.
GV956.6.A27   1984   796.332′72   83-22193
ISBN 0-8225-1556-3 (lib. bdg.)

1 2 3 4 5 6 7 8 9 10 93 92 91 90 89 88 87 86 85 84

CONTENTS

	Become the Coach!	5
1	Four Yards and a Cloud of Dust	7
2	Time Is On Your Side—Isn't It?	16
3	Surprise!	24
4	One Yard Away from a Perfect Season	36
5	Go for Two!	44
6	Break the Wishbone!	56
7	Keeping Up with the Joneses (and Smiths, and Washingtons...)	66
8	Rising Tide	76
9	Night of the Defense	84
10	"How 'Bout Them Dawgs!"	94

Become the Coach!

It's New Year's Day, and college football fans across the country are set to relax and enjoy the big college bowl games. It's too bad you can't join them in the stands, but it's a work day for you. There's no such thing as a holiday when <u>you</u> are the coach.

College football coaches must face many tough decisions in their careers, but few experience anything more challenging than the problems that come up in a bowl game. These games are big affairs with strong traditions dating back many years: the first Cotton Bowl game was played back in 1937, the Sugar Bowl in 1935, the Orange Bowl in 1933, and the Rose Bowl all the way back in 1902. What happens in these games will go down in sports history. Will you be remembered as the coach whose daring and cleverness won the game? Or will you be the one who blew it?

If you make a call that turns out wrong, there's no place for you to hide. As many as 100,000 people will be on hand watching <u>you</u>, millions more will tune in on television, and network broadcasters won't be shy about pointing out your mistake. They're going to demand to know <u>why</u> you did what you did, especially if it cost you the game.

This book puts you on the sidelines at ten of the most exciting bowl games ever played. As coach, you will have to beat some of the finest teams and players of the last 20 years. Bubba Smith, Tommy Nobis, Gene Washington, Dwight Stephenson, Tony Nathan, and Dan Marino present you with some baffling problems. You're going to have to decide what to do when:

• You face a fourth down at your opponent's one-yard line, trailing by four points.

• You face a Texas offense that has averaged nearly 400 yards a game.

• You're stuck with a third down and 8 on your own 2-yard line, leading by one point in the final minute of the game.

Sometimes you will have to coach an overmatched team. At other times you must deal with the pressure of trying to hold onto your number-one ranking. Either way, you will find that even the "unimportant" plays, such as field goals, kickoffs, and extra points, will leave you with a headache.

Read your close-up scouting reports carefully to get as much information as possible. You will need all the help you can get as you prepare to ring in the New Year with a big win. See how you compare with some of the best coaches in college football. It's your move, coach!

1 Four Yards and a Cloud of Dust

You are coaching the Ohio State University Buckeyes.

This New Year's Day, 1969, your number-one-rated Buckeyes are locked in a gripping duel with the second-ranked Trojans of the University of Southern California (USC). Your team has a 13-10 lead.

It's early in the fourth quarter, and your defense has forced a turnover that could wrap up this Rose Bowl win.

Clever running by quarterback Rex Kern has put you inside the USC five. Unfortunately, it is now third down, your ground attack is stalling, and you still have four yards to go to get into the end zone.

You need a touchdown for a comfortable margin over the Trojans. How will you get it? Before choosing the play, consider the following facts about both teams.

Close-up:
The USC Defense

The Trojans have been winning games with their offense, not their defense. It's been like a revolving door at some defensive positions as they have shuffled men in and out trying to find the best players. In this game, they have been forced by injuries to make some changes in their line. USC has switched its best defensive lineman, 6-foot, 5-inch, 255-pound Al Cowlings, from tackle to right end. Middle guard Willard Scott has moved to tackle, and Bill Redding has taken over at middle guard.

This shuffle has given USC a lineup far larger than yours and is one reason that you've had to work hard for running yards today. The other reason is that USC linebacker Jim Snow has frequently shown up in the right spot to ruin Buckeye plays. USC's defensive backfield has no big-name stars and has not had an outstanding day. Obviously, they've been concentrating on stopping your power running game.

Al Cowlings

Willard Scott

Close-Up:
Ohio State Offense

Sophomore quarterback Rex Kern leads your offense. Although one of the youngest players on the field, he is also one of the calmest. Kern had the nerve this season to wave the punting team off the field after you had ordered them into the game! Then he backed up his daring deed by running for a first down.

Kern is not the classic tall drop-back passer admired by the pros. But he has shown that he can throw the ball, and he has two fine receivers in Jan White and Bruce Jankowski. Rex does even better as a runner and ranked second on the team in rushing.

A confident Rex Kern issues orders to his offense.

Ordinarily, your team excels at scoring from close in. In fact, writers have often referred to your offense as "three yards and a cloud of dust." This means that you like to blast straight ahead for small, steady gains rather than risk passes or trick plays.

The Buckeyes' top runner has been 6-foot-tall, 200-pound workhorse Jim Otis. Quick off the mark for a big man, this human battering ram bursts into the line before opponents can fight off their blockers. In a game against Michigan earlier this season, he gained 143 yards and scored four touchdowns. In this game, both Otis and Kern are averaging only about three yards per try.

Your other top backs are Larry Zelina and Leo Hayden. Both are all-around performers, with Zelina having more speed and Hayden more strength. Zelina played more in the regular season, but Hayden has been enjoying the best game of his career. He is averaging about six yards per carry and is drawing close to 100 yards.

An excellent group of blockers leads the way for these runners. Few other coaches have enjoyed the luxury of starting two All-American tackles at either side of the offensive line like you have. Dave Foley and Rufus Mayes have provided much of the muscle for your ground attack. Occasionally you have placed them side by side to form an awesome blocking wedge. The center of your line, however, is outweighed by USC's huge linemen.

OSU YARDS RUSHING		**OSU YARDS PASSING**	
Otis	985	Kern	972
Kern	534		
Zelina	338		
Hayden	284		

Leo Hayden

Rufus Mayes

You should also consider what will happen if you fail to score on this play. Jim Roman is available to kick a field goal for you, but you will make his job harder if you run a play toward the sidelines. Because the ball will then be placed near where the play is stopped, not in the center of the field, Roman could be forced to kick at a difficult angle.

What's Your Decision?

> You are the coach.
> You need four yards, but your ground attack is stalling. Will you continue to rely on your run, or try something else?
> **What play will you call?**
>
> #1 Put Foley and Mayes on the same side and have Otis blast through behind them.
>
> #2 Have Kern run to the right with the option of pitching to Zelina who is trailing the play.
>
> #3 Fake a running play into the line; have Kern run to the left and pass to Hayden.
>
> #4 Have Kern drop straight back to pass to either White or Jankowski.

Choose the play. Then turn the page to see which play the Ohio State coach chose.

Ohio State tried #3.

It's tough to gain yards when you get close to the goal line. Few teams can expect to gain four yards on a running play so near the end zone (#1, #2). It would be especially difficult for Kern or Otis, since USC seems to be concentrating on them.

Kern is not exceptional as a pure passer, though, and Ohio State's passing game is not particularly strong (#4). The Buckeyes felt they could best use Kern's athletic skill by having him throw on the run. A fake run into the line and a rollout should draw the Trojans out of position. That might allow the relatively unknown Hayden, who is playing well, to sneak into the end zone to catch the pass.

Here's What Happened!

At the snap of the ball, the Ohio State line surged ahead, as usual. Kern faked a handoff up the middle and sprinted to his left. Aware that Kern was a dangerous runner and that it was difficult for a right-hander like Kern to throw while running left, USC came up to force the play. Meanwhile, Hayden quietly worked his way into the corner of the end zone behind the Trojan backs. Kern was able to toss accurately to the unguarded Hayden for the touchdown.

That play put the Buckeyes ahead 20-10. Against the Buckeyes' talented young defense, even tough USC could not close that gap. Forced to play an unfamiliar style of catch-up ball, USC fell behind 27-10 before finally losing 27-16. With the victory, Ohio State was able to claim the nation's number-one spot.

Buckeye Rex Kern (10) is shown here breaking tackles in one of his many running plays of the day. The day's surprise, though, was Kern's accurate pass to Hayden, which sealed Ohio State's win.

2 Time Is On Your Side—Isn't It?

Can your stubborn Penn State defense, here crunching Alabama's Jeff Rutledge, get the ball back for your offense with enough time to break up a scoreless first half?

You are coaching the Penn State Nittany Lions.

Your unbeaten squad has fought to a scoreless draw against Alabama in this 1979 Sugar Bowl. The second-ranked Crimson Tide of Coach Bear Bryant is clearly after your number-one ranking, and they have outplayed you throughout the first half. Bottled up in your own end of the field, you've been unable to do anything on offense.

Now you have finally broken Alabama's grip and have sent them deep into their end of the field. They have the ball on their 20-yard line with 1:11 remaining in the half. That is not much time for them to march into scoring position against your magnificent defense.

Do you want to gamble that your defense can stop Alabama before they get a first down? This would force them to punt, giving you possession of the ball. If you want to gamble, you should use your time-outs to stop the clock while you are on defense. This would give your offense time to take advantage of good field position for a possible field goal before halftime. If your defense does <u>not</u> stop Alabama, though, your time-outs may give them the extra time <u>they</u> need to score.

Or will you play it safe, let the Crimson Tide run out the clock, and settle for a 0-0 tie at halftime?

Close-Up:
The Alabama Offense

While playing Alabama, you have had the uneasy feeling that they have you outnumbered. They have shuffled fresh players into the game with little drop-off in talent. Among their host of fine running backs are Tony Nathan and Major Ogilvie. Nathan, a quick back with sure hands, is a smart open-field runner. Ogilvie's driving style brings consistent gains rather than big plays.

Don't be fooled by the fact that Alabama prefers to run the ball. The present quarterback, Jeff Rutledge, has been playing in the rich tradition of Crimson Tide quarterbacks that started with Joe Namath and Ken Stabler. Rutledge recently broke Namath's career record of 28 touchdown passes. Rutledge is a master at drawing linebackers in close with a running fake and then whistling a long pass to wide receivers like Bruce Bolton.

Led by explosive center Dwight Stephenson, the blocking for both Rutledge and the running backs has been impressive. As a result, Alabama has moved the ball surprisingly well at times.

Jeff Rutledge

Major Ogilvie

Bruce Bolton

Dwight Stephenson

Close-Up:
The Penn State Defense

Your defense deserves most of the credit for your 19-game winning streak. They are considered the best major college unit in the country. This season they have given up only 203 yards per game. An even more impressive statistic is that they have allowed fewer than 55 yards rushing per game!

The main reason for this stinginess is that opposing runners keep banging into two 260-pound All-American tackles, Bruce Clark and Matt Millen. These men seal off the middle of the field while such players as Lance Mehl and Rich Milot mop up the rest.

Matt Millen

Bruce Clark

Lance Mehl

Rich Milot

Your pass rush has forced quarterbacks into throwing dangerous passes. That has helped your inexperienced defensive backs grab 28 interceptions this year. Although Pete Harris (brother of Franco, Pittsburgh Steeler great) is a fine safety, the defensive backfield is not as good as the rest of the unit. The only top quarterback they have faced this year is Mike Ford of Southern Methodist University, who passed for 289 yards against them. Rutledge is considered at least as good as Ford.

In the past, your team has risen to the occasion in tough games. You came up with five interceptions and held number-five-rated Maryland to negative 32 yards rushing in an important 27-3 win. Can you count on your Nittany Lions to stop Alabama's offense in the next three plays?

What's Your Decision?

You are the coach.
Can your defense hold Alabama and give your polished quarterback, Chuck Fusina, a chance to score before halftime?
What do you tell your defensive captain?

#1 Risk calling a time out.
#2 Play it safe and let the clock run out.

Choose your strategy. Then turn the page to find out which strategy the Penn State coach chose.

Penn State selected option #1.

Based on the fine play of his defense over the season, Penn State coach Joe Paterno felt that he could count on them to get the ball back for his offense. In a low-scoring game like this, three points could easily decide the game. Penn State chose to stop the clock in hopes of getting the ball back in time to earn a field goal and a 3-0 lead.

Here's What Happened!

Twice Penn State stopped the clock, only to watch Alabama roll to a first down. Once they had moved out from deep in their own end, the Crimson Tide realized they had enough time left to try for a score of their own.

As Penn State backers looked on in frustration, Rutledge's quick passes sped his team quickly downfield. With enough time left for one or two more plays, Alabama reached the Penn State 30, just within field goal range. The Tide, though, was growing more confident with each play, and they decided a field goal wasn't enough. Disguising his play well, Rutledge sent Bruce Bolton racing toward the end zone. With only eight seconds left in the half, Bolton dove and caught the pass for the touchdown.

Alabama later held off Penn State on a crucial fourth-down run from inside the one-yard line. They hung on to win the game, 14-7, and snatched the number-one rating from the Nittany Lions. Before Penn State called those two fateful time-outs, Alabama had been content to run out the clock. Instead, they were nudged into a touchdown march that proved to be the margin of victory.

Where Penn State's defense failed, Alabama's prevailed. Here they stop Matt Suhey inside the one-yard line.

3 Surprise!

Michigan wasn't laughing when Stanford back Jackie Brown fooled them by turning a fake punt into a 31-yard run.

You are coaching the Stanford University Indians.

On the first play of this 1972 Rose Bowl, you tried a reverse handoff kickoff return. That bit of razzle-dazzle didn't fool the Michigan Wolverines, but it did signal to the fans that this game would be full of surprises.

Since then, you've tried every trick you can think of to outwit the powerful, favored Wolverines. Your most recent attempt still has the Michigan coaching staff blushing. Trailing 10-3, your offense failed to make a yard in three downs and went into punt formation. Michigan failed to see until it was too late, however, that Stanford wasn't kicking! Running back Jackie Brown scampered for 31 easy yards before the Wolverines finally recovered and hauled him down.

All of this trickery has added up to the biggest surprise of all—the fact that the score is still tied at 10-10 with less than four minutes remaining. But this fast and loose play may finally have caught up with you. A few moments ago you lost your fourth fumble of the game, which Michigan recovered on your 35. Fortunately, linebacker Jeff Siemon and his mates held the Wolverines' strong running attack to six yards in three tries and then forced them to try for a field goal.

Michigan's kicker, Dana Coin, has set his kicking block at the 36. Since the goalposts stand 10 yards beyond the goal line, that makes it a 46-yard attempt. This distance is near the limit of Coin's accurate kicking range.

The way this game is going, a field goal here could decide the game. How will you prepare your defense? You have three choices to consider.

#1: You could go for the block.

You could mass your players at the line for an all-out rush to block the kick. You certainly don't want to give away three points this late in a tie game if you can possibly help it. If you think you can block it, you probably should. A good block not only prevents a possible score, but it can give you good field position to start your own game-winning drive. The only risks involved are that an overeager player may be penalized for jumping offside or that Michigan might try a trick play.

#2: You could play it safe and guard against the fake.

You aren't the only team allowed to spring surprises in this game. After what you did to them on that fourth-down fake earlier, Michigan would like nothing better than to catch your team napping.

With the ball on your 29-yard line, Michigan can afford to gamble. If you send too many men in to block the kick, they could toss a pass right over you. The result could be either a touchdown or another chance for Michigan's grinding offense to move in for a time-consuming score. You can't expect Siemon and company to hold off Michigan's all-time rushing leader, Billy Taylor, or his All-American guard, Reggie McKenzie, forever.

Billy Taylor

Reggie McKenzie

There's a reasonable chance that Coin will miss from that range, so it may be safer just to let him kick. If he misses, you get the ball at your 20 with a chance to launch a game-winning drive. Even if he makes it, you would be only three points down with plenty of time left to score.

DANA COIN'S SEASON RECORD

Point After Touchdown		Field Goal	
Attempts	**Made**	**Attempts**	**Made**
55	55	14	8

Stanford quarterback Don Bunce has upheld his team's tradition of fine passers.

Remember that your quarterback, Don Bunce, has played so well today that you hardly miss last season's star, Jim Plunkett. Bunce throws well and is an excellent option runner, a combination that put him second in the country in total offense. His receivers, such as John Winesberry, have been able to break loose despite the presence of All American Tom Darden in the Wolverine defensive backfield. You may want to play it safe on this kick and leave it to your offense to make up for any points scored by Michigan.

#3: You could also try to run back the kick.

Although you rarely see it done, field goal attempts that are unsuccessful may be run back by the defending team. On this 46-yard kick, there is at least a chance that the kick will be returnable. You have tricked Michigan before with an unexpected play; you might be able to slip back a player who can race downfield before the Wolverines figure out what is happening.

This would be a big gamble in hopes of a big play. If Michigan reacts well to the play, you probably won't make it to your 20. That would make it tough on your offense, which would have to break out of its own end against Michigan All Americans Mike Taylor and Tom Darden. If you do get a big gain out of it, though, it will give a boost to your offense.

#1. Mass defense on line to block kick.

```
         O
       O
   O oooooooo O
  X  X   X X X X X X    X X
              X
```

O Offense
X Defense

#2. Hold back some players to guard against trick plays.

```
            O
          O
   O oooooooo O
  X   X   X X X X   X X
      X        X        X
```

O Offense
X Defense

30

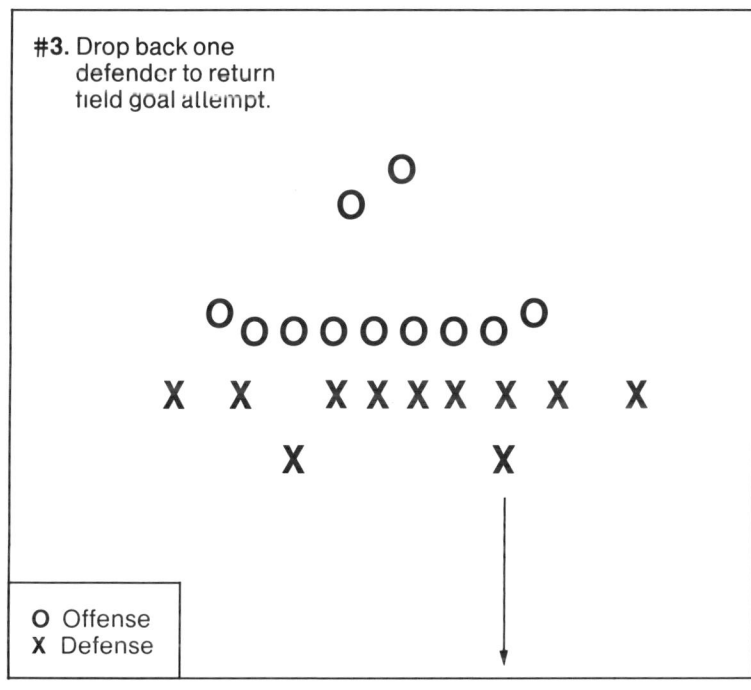

#3. Drop back one defender to return field goal attempt.

O Offense
X Defense

What's Your Decision?

You are the coach.
Michigan has sent their regular kicking unit into the game. Will they kick?
What will you do?

#1 Go for the block.
#2 Lay back and watch for tricks.
#3 Set up a possible return.

Choose the play. Then turn the page to find out what play the Stanford coach chose.

Stanford tried #3.

Stanford coach John Ralston was not convinced that his team could get through to block the kick (#1). As he had done throughout the game, he decided to gamble and try to force his own breaks. Stanford was not under crushing pressure to win, so they felt free to try some unusual tricks. Ralston sent instructions to defensive back Jim Ferguson to drop back and run with the ball if the kick was short.

Here's What Happened!

Michigan was not fooling around; they all stayed in to block for their kicker. Coin, who had already kicked one field goal in the game, did not get off a solid kick. Seeing that the ball would fall well short of the goal posts, Stanford's Ferguson moved into position to catch it. Fielding the ball near his goal line, the sophomore started upfield. He made it only as far as the six when he ran into the first wave of alert Michigan defenders. Trying to sprint away from them into the open field, Ferguson peeled back in an arc toward his goal. He could not get clear of Wolverine fullback Ed Shuttlesworth, however, and was knocked back into his end zone.

The stunned Stanford fans, who had been grinning over Michigan's missed field goal, could hardly believe what they had just seen. Their team had just given away two crucial points on a needless safety! Not only were they behind now, 12-10, but Stanford had to kick off from their own 20 with three minutes to go in the game.

Fortunately, Stanford's defense stopped three straight running plays by the conservative Wolverines and got the ball back with 1:48 left to play. Throwing at will against the Wolverines, Bunce hustled his team upfield all the way to Michigan's 14. With only 12 seconds left in the game, Rod Garcia came out to try a 31-yard field goal. This time Garcia was on target. His kick gave Stanford a 13-12 upset win and saved the Stanford coaches from humiliation over their enormous blunder.

The winning kick was *not* made by Dana Coin but by Stanford kicker Rod Garcia, who saved the day by booting this 31-yard field goal.

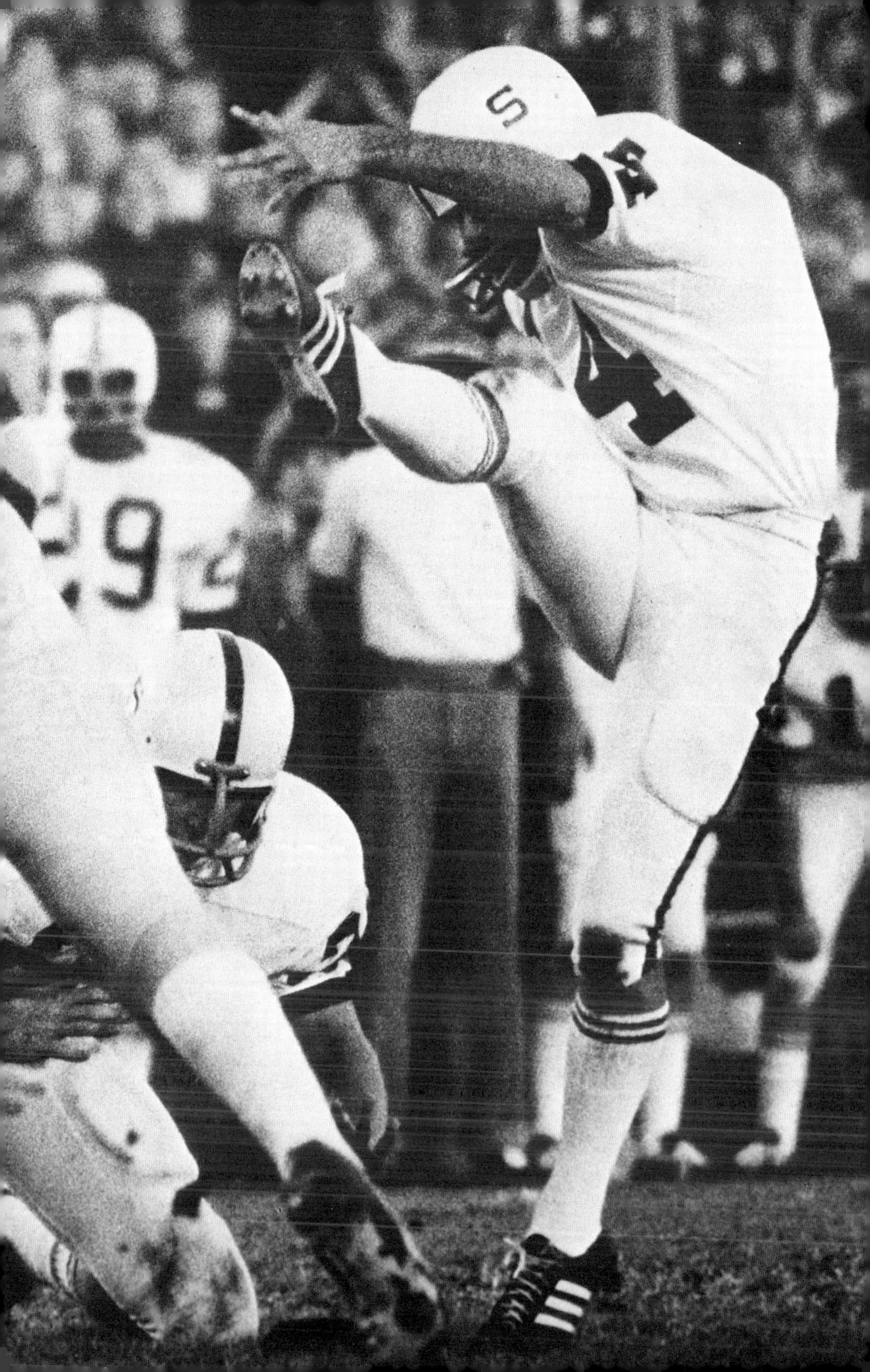
29

4 One Yard Away from a Perfect Season

Joe Namath passes for an Alabama touchdown as the Crimson Tide makes its comeback in this exciting Orange Bowl contest.

You are coaching the University of Alabama Crimson Tide.

The University of Texas Longhorns have joined you in making sure that this first nighttime Orange Bowl game won't put anyone to sleep. The Longhorns treated fans to a 69-yard touchdown pass and a 79-yard touchdown run in grabbing a 21-7 first-half lead. In the second half of this 1965 contest, however, your unbeaten, number-one-ranked team has taken over.

Injured quarterback Joe Namath has led your heroic comeback in closing the gap to 21-17 late in the fourth quarter. Now Namath has Alabama on the move again with a first down at the Texas six. A knot is starting to grow in your stomach as you watch fullback Steve Bowman carry on three straight plays for four yards, no gain, and one yard respectively. That's left you just one yard short of the goal line.

Time is running out, and a field goal will do you no good. You need a touchdown or you can forget about your dreams of an unbeaten season. How will you score?

37

Close-Up:
The Texas Defense

The Longhorns are a conservative team. They play their basic positions on defense with little experimentation. As you can tell from the last three plays, Texas plays well against the run. They take pride in their number-six ranking nationally against rushing attacks. If you needed any further proof of their stubbornness, Texas gave it to you in the first quarter. You tried to play without Namath's passing arm and did not get a single first down in the quarter.

The Longhorns have tough, strong linemen such as Diron Talbert. But the biggest roadblock in the way of your touchdown is junior linebacker Tommy Nobis. Already he's being compared to Illinois' ferocious Dick Butkus as one of the most punishing tacklers in the game.

Against this defense, you've had far better success passing than running. But down near the goal line there is not much room for your receivers to run their patterns. This means you will have to consider various other options in choosing your play.

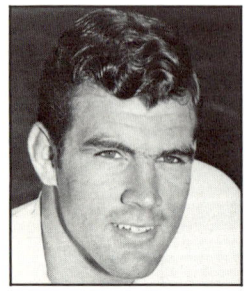

Diron Talbert

Tommy Nobis

Close-Up:
The Alabama Offense

Joe Namath is one of those super athletes who can do whatever you ask of him in a game—when he's healthy, that is. Right now he is not. Ever since he hurt his right knee in the fourth game on your schedule, Joe has been struggling. While practicing the week before this game, Namath hurt his knee again, and you were afraid he wouldn't be able to play. But the Longhorns' impressive first half forced you to press him into service to see if he could save the game.

No sooner did Namath step onto the field than your offense came to life. Joe's passes produced all but 4 of the 87 yards on your first touchdown drive. Since then, he has continued to bomb the Longhorns with two more scoring drives, and now this threat on the Texas one-yard line.

Although he's a reserve for Alabama, quarterback Steve Sloan is good enough to start for most college teams. He has kept your unbeaten record intact by filling in several times for the injured Namath. Although Sloan has a sore leg of his own, he could give you a scoring option that Namath could not. Your team has some special quarterback option plays designed for the more agile Sloan. This has not been a shining evening for Sloan, however. He was the one in charge of your offense during its miserable first quarter.

Although your team is rated number one, you don't have any other players who could really be considered stars. Speedy Ray Perkins leads a lengthy list of pass receivers who can catch the ball well. Your backfield is stocked with two powerful backs, Steve Bowman and Leslie Kelley. Although both are hard-nosed 200-pounders, neither has that outstanding quickness that would help you run to the outside. Bowman has made only four feet on his last two carries combined.

Clockwise from top left: Les Kelley, Ray Perkins, Steve Sloan

Perhaps one of the reasons you have trouble running against Texas is that you have one of the smallest blocking lines in college football. Most of your blockers are not even as large as your running backs. Ordinarily, they make up for their size with quickness, but that hasn't helped much today.

Steve Bowman

What's Your Decision?

You are the coach.
It's late in the fourth quarter and you're trailing by four points.
What play will you devise to get that last yard and a touchdown?

#1 Send Bowman up the middle again.

#2 Replace Namath with Sloan; run a rollout where Sloan can choose to pass, run, or pitch out to a back.

#3 Run Namath on a quarterback sneak.

#4 Have Namath try a pass.

Choose the play. Then turn the page to find out which play the Alabama coach chose.

Alabama went with #3.

Namath had shown that he was far better with one good leg than most quarterbacks are with two. Rather than put in Sloan (#2), Alabama wanted to stick with their best player because Namath had a knack of finding ways to win. Being only a yard away, the Crimson Tide chose to play it safe with another run rather than a pass (#4). Bowman had not been getting anywhere on his last carries and would have been an even greater risk (#1). Alabama hoped that a quick sneak by the quarterback would surprise the Longhorns. All Namath had to do was lunge forward, so there was little chance that his injured leg would be a problem.

Here's What Happened!

Namath thought he saw just enough room in the Longhorn line to slip past them into the end zone. Taking the snap from center, he wormed his way behind his blockers toward the goal line. Longhorn Tommy Nobis reacted quickly, though, and met Namath head on. After Namath disappeared under a huge pile of players, he reappeared, excitedly clutching the ball in the end zone.

The officials ruled that he had been stopped, however, and that the whistle had blown before he had squirmed across the line. No touchdown signal was given and the ball was turned over to Texas. Namath could not believe that he was not awarded a touchdown. He and other players complained about the call but could not change it.

When asked if the quarterback sneak was the right call to make, Alabama coach Bear Bryant commented wryly that he might have called for something else if he had been allowed ten days to think about it. As it was, that unsuccessful sneak bumped his team from the unbeaten ranks as Texas held on to a 21-17 win.

Coach Bear Bryant and Joe Namath show their pain after being defeated by Texas.

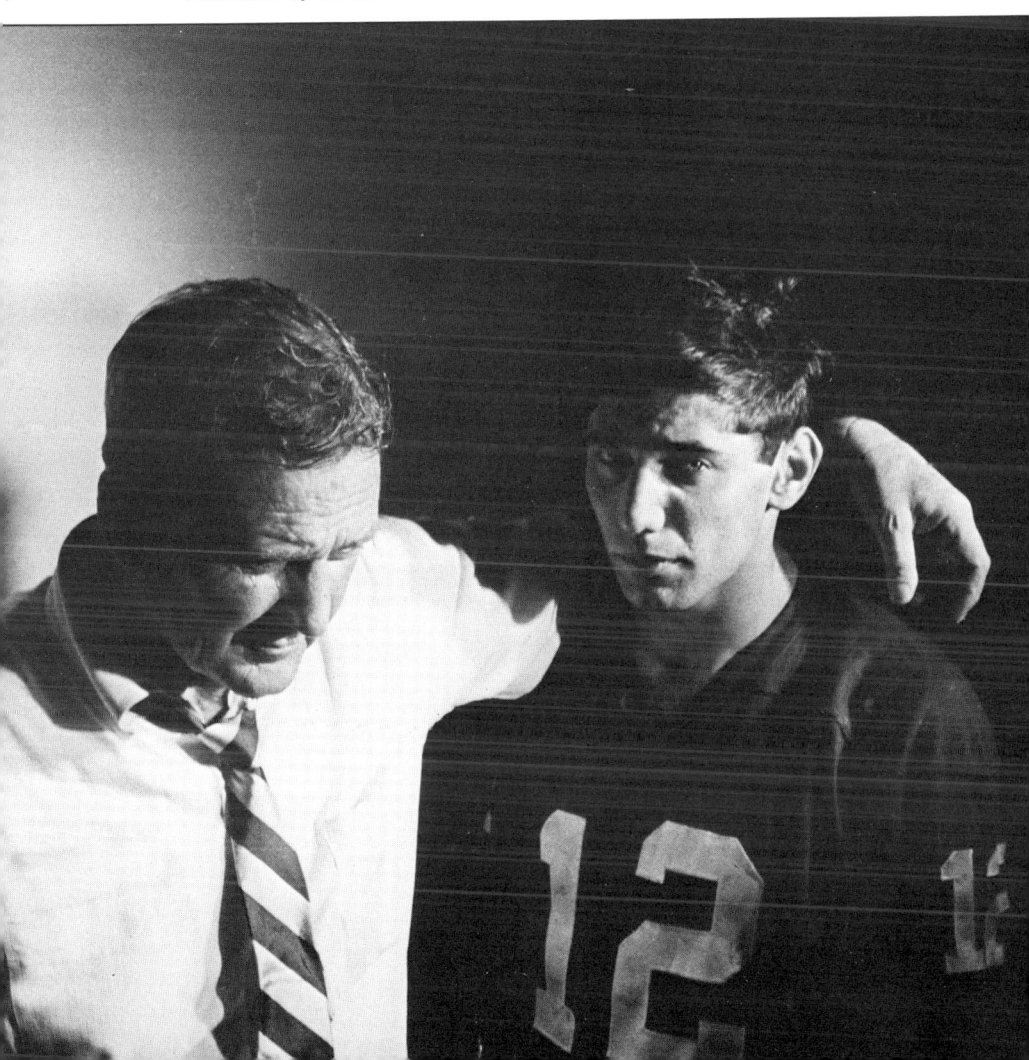

5 Go For Two!

With time running out, Penn State's Bobby Campbell races goalward with a 47-yard Chuck Burkhart pass before getting dragged down at the three-yard line by Kansas safety Tom Anderson.

You are coaching the Penn State Nittany Lions.

   Until the final minute of play, this 1969 Orange Bowl was not one of your more exciting contests. You have spent most of the low-scoring game scrambling to avoid certain defeat at the hands of the University of Kansas Jayhawks. Fortunately, luck is wearing a Penn State uniform in this second half. Your 10-man rush got a piece of a Jayhawk punt, which rolled only as far as their 49-yard line.
   With 1:20 left to play, Penn State running back Bobby Campbell somehow wrestled away a long pass from your opponents for a gain all the way to the three! Finally, after two running plays failed, your offense scored on a messed-up play. Quarterback Chuck Burkhart was supposed to pitch the ball to running back Charlie Pittman. But a Kansas defender got between the two and Burkhart had to keep the ball. He surprised everyone by scoring his first running touchdown of the year!
   That brings you to within one point of Kansas. At 14-13, you could easily tie the game by kicking the extra point. But this is a major college bowl game, and fans and players are pleading with you to go for the two-point conversion. What will you do?

45

Close-Up:
The Kansas Defense

This game was expected to pit the Jayhawks' offensive stars Bobby Douglass, John Riggins, and Donnie Shanklin against your defense. But Kansas has shown it can play defense as well. They have allowed only 175 points this season and held a good Nebraska team to only 13 points in the Cornhuskers' own stadium. And they had kept your team well under control in this game, too, until you turned the tide in the last minute.

Kansas has packed their defensive line with massive players. You are not going to get far in a test of muscles against 260-pound Vernon Vanoy or 275-pound world-class shot putter Karl Salb. While 235-pound end John Zook seems almost small in comparison to Vanoy and Salb, he is an even more effective lineman. His pass-rushing skills have helped him to earn All-American honors. This Jayhawk line has held firm on the last few downs, making the three yards you need for the two-point conversion seem like an ocean away.

The Kansas linebackers are good, but not great. They come in all sizes, ranging from 232-pound Emery Hicks to 167-pound Pat Hutchens, but none has earned national recognition. The defensive backs are not household names either, but they have played well today. Before that last lapse against Campbell, they had allowed only 108 yards passing and had stolen two Penn State throws.

Vernon Vanoy

Karl Salb

John Zook

Close-Up:
The Penn State Offense

Penn State's scoring average of 34 points per game seems to show that you have a high-powered attack. But when you look at the fine print, you'll see that it was your <u>defense</u> that scored over a third of those points. In fact, your defense scored more points than it allowed!

The missing ingredient in your attack is probably a top quarterback. Chuck Burkhart does not run the ball well, and he's no wizard at passing, either. His season totals of 87 completions in 177 attempts for 1,170 yards aren't bad, but these figures won't get him into any record books. This game has been about average for him with 12 completions in 23 throws, good for 152 yards. Those two interceptions that he threw have hurt. Despite his drawbacks, though, Chuck is a good offensive leader with a knack for winning.

Chuck Burkhart

Burkhart is lucky to have a large and visible target in tight end Ted Kwalick. With speed and coordination to go with his 6-foot, 4-inch, 230-pound size, Ted is certain to become a pro star. Half of tonight's 12 pass completions have wound up in his hands.

Running back Bobby Campbell is the one most responsible for giving you a chance to win this game. A high school sprint and high jump champ, he may be the finest athlete you have ever coached. Although bothered by injuries in his career, he has shown flashes of brilliance. You remember well the 207 yards he gained in one half against a highly rated Syracuse team. In this game he has rushed for 102 yards on 18 carries, and he has caught two passes for 55 more yards.

Ted Kwalick   Charlie Pittman

Bobby Campbell (23) has been in top form in this Orange Bowl and has contributed 157 yards so far.

Campbell has shared the Penn State running load with another fine back, Charlie Pittman. A durable, consistent back, Pittman averaged over five yards per carry during the year and scored 14 touchdowns. He has continued to crack into the end zone tonight with a 13-yard scamper for your first touchdown. His 61 yards in 16 runs does not come close to Campbell's performance, however. Fullback Tom Cherry provides some extra power for short yardage situations, but he was stopped for no gain on his last two carries.

What's Your Decision?

You are the coach.
You are three yards away from the end zone, and you need those two points to win the game.
How will you get them?

#1 Send out running back Campbell for a pass.
#2 Let Pittman carry the ball on an off-tackle play.
#3 Fire a quick pass to Kwalick.
#4 Give the ball to Campbell on a sweep around the end.

Choose the play. Then turn the page to find out which play the Penn State coach chose.

Penn State sent play #1 into the huddle.

Three yards was too far to run against the big Kansas goal-line defense (#2, #4). Of the remaining choices, coach Joe Paterno decided to go with the player who was hot. Campbell had fought through the Kansas defenders to make a great catch under nearly impossible conditions to set up the score. If he could do it once, maybe he could do it again.

Here's What Happened!

When Burkhart dropped back to pass, his receivers seemed like small dots in the middle of the Jayhawk huddle. When he could wait no longer, he threw towards Campbell and hoped that Bobby could somehow come up with it. But a swarm of Kansas players batted down the pass.

Kansas players had seemed to be all over the end zone, and it turned out there was a good reason for that. The Jayhawks had accidently been playing with 12 defenders instead of 11. The heartbroken Nittany Lions perked up when they saw that they would get another chance to win the game.

The officials have placed the ball half the distance to the goal line, at the 1½, and ordered the down replayed. A running play now has a better chance of working. It's time to make another quick decision.

What play do you call this time?

#1 Send Campbell out for another pass.
#2 Send Pittman off tackle.
#3 Throw a quick pass to Kwalick.
#4 Send Campbell around end.
#5 Let Burkhart carry with an option to run or pass.

Choose the running play. Then turn the page to find out which play the Penn State coach chose.

This time Penn State tried #4.

Now that they were within running distance of the goal line, Penn State was happy to set aside their unimpressive passing game (#1, #3, #5). Campbell was still the man they wanted to use. His speed might allow him to outsprint the Kansas defenders to the corner of the end zone. That seemed a better risk than challenging the size and power of the Kansas line (#2).

Here's What Happened!

What a difference a yard and a half can make! Campbell sped toward the left sideline and crossed the goal line ahead of the Kansas defenders. Many coaches wish that they could get a second chance when a decision doesn't work out. Joe Paterno was one of the lucky ones who did. Thanks to some sloppy counting on the part of the Jayhawks, Paterno was able to erase an unsuccessful play and start all over with a new one. Because of this fluke error, Penn State claimed an unforgettable 15-14 win.

A grateful Bobby Campbell signals
his joy after scoring the winning points.

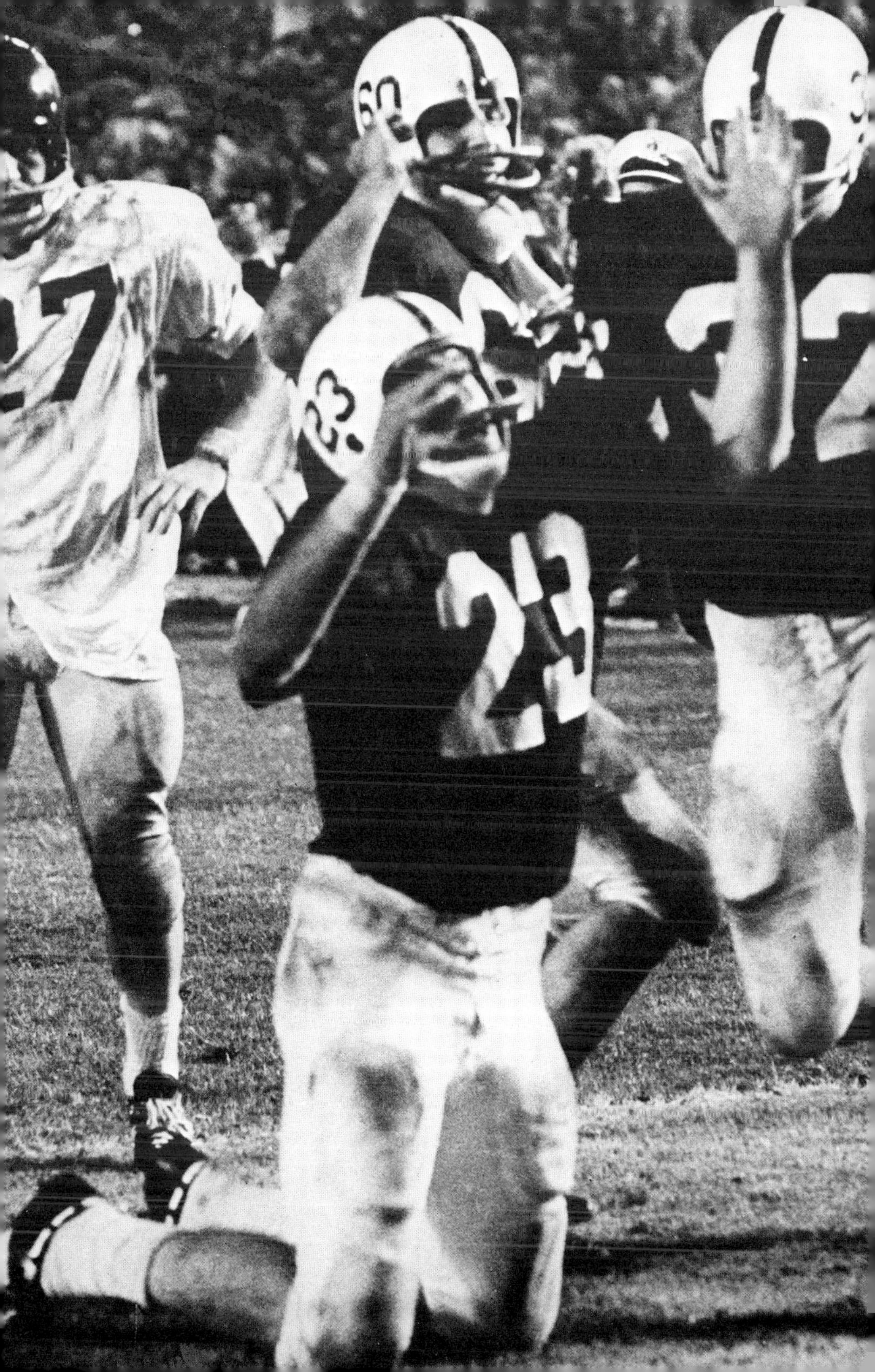

6 Break the Wishbone!

Three tough prongs in the Longhorn wishbone: running backs Steve Worster (left) and Jim Bertelsen, and quarterback Eddie Phillips. If the Irish are to have their luck, the wishbone must be snapped.

You are coaching the Notre Dame Fighting Irish.

If you are looking for revenge, this return match of last year's Cotton Bowl may be a poor way to get it. This Texas Longhorn team is even stronger than the one that beat you 21-17 in the 1970 Cotton Bowl. The Longhorns, everyone's choice as the top team in the country, bring a 30-game winning streak into this 1971 affair.

Texas has been unstoppable ever since they perfected their "wishbone" offense. No one has yet figured out a way to slow down, much less stop, the explosive running attack. Your sixth-ranked Irish must come up with a plan to defeat the Longhorns' running attack or else this game will be a rerun of last year's Cotton Bowl defeat. What will you do?

Close-Up:
The Texas Offense

The Texas offense is called a wishbone formation because of the way the backfield lines up. The fullback moves forward, turning a "T" formation into a wishbone (see diagram). Almost every play run out of this formation is a triple option. That is, the quarterback has the option of handing off to the fullback straight ahead, carrying the ball off tackle, or pitching out to a back around end. If executed properly, it forces the defense to tackle all three men to make sure they've stopped the man who has the ball.

The Texas Wishbone Triple Option:
#1: Quarterback (1) may hand off to fullback (2), who runs off guard. **#2:** Quarterback (1) may fake a handoff, keep the ball, and run off tackle. **#3:** Quarterback (1) may pitch the ball to halfback (3), who will run around end while the other halfback (4) leads the blocking.

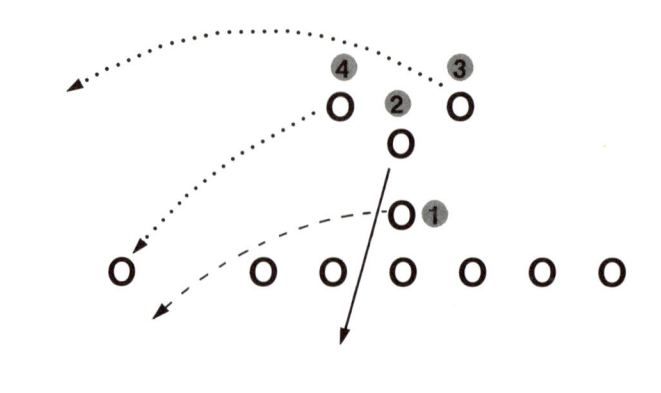

In winning all ten games this season, the Longhorns <u>averaged</u> 41 points and 374 yards rushing per game. The leading man on this veteran club is fullback Steve Worster. A three-year starter, Worster was the runner who destroyed you last year with 155 yards in 20 carries. This year the steady senior again led Texas in both rushing and scoring, with 898 yards and 14 touchdowns. His job in the wishbone is to break tackles in the middle of the line.

Stopping Worster's power is not your only task, however. Improved halfback Jim Bertelsen has added balance and speed to the Longhorn attack. He has outsprinted defenders around the ends for 891 yards and 13 touchdowns.

The middle man in the operation is quarterback Eddie Phillips. Wishbone quarterbacks have to run the ball, and Eddie has chipped in with 666 yards and 12 touchdowns. He has never been tested as a passer, simply because Texas has rarely found a reason to pass. Averaging fewer than 10 passes per game, Phillips has completed less than half of them. But when he has connected, he has made it count with a 17.8-yard-per-completion average.

With these three in the main wishbone positions, all that Texas asks of the other eight players is that they block. A veteran and improved Texas line has come through in that department 30 games in a row.

Close-Up:
The Notre Dame Defense

In last year's Cotton Bowl, the Longhorns rolled up 381 rushing yards against a Notre Dame defense led by Mike McCoy and Bob Olson. If those stars couldn't stop Texas, what will you do now that they are gone?

On the bright side, your usual supply of enormous young defensive linemen has come up to fill the graduation gaps. Greg Marx and Mike Kadish combine to give you over 520 pounds of power at the tackle spots. Six-foot, five-inch, 250-pound end Walt Patulski excels at spoiling plays to his side of the field. The Irish also have plenty of beefy linemen in reserve.

Greg Marx   Mike Kadish

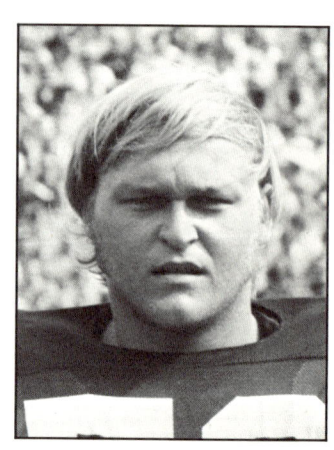

This year you have no linebackers the quality of Olson, but Clarence Ellis gives you outstanding play at defensive back. His All-American pass-defending skills, however, may be wasted against a running team like Texas.

What's Your Decision?

You are the coach.
No one has come close to stopping the wishbone attack this year.
What defense can you use to stop Worster's power, Bertelsen's speed, and Phillips' cleverness?

#1 Play your usual defense. Count on your burly linemen to improve on last year's play.

#2 Dare Texas to pass. Put eight men near the line of scrimmage lined up in a mirror image of the wishbone formation.

#3 Send Clarence Ellis on blitzes from his cornerback spot to upset the plays before they start.

#4 Bring in an extra defensive lineman to overpower the Texas line.

Choose the defense. Then turn the page to find out which defense the Notre Dame coach used.

Notre Dame chose plan #2.

Irish coach Ara Parseghian had seen that normal defenses could not cope with all the wishbone options (#1). The only way to stop this offense was to stop everyone in the backfield. In order to do that, Notre Dame needed more players close to the line. Notre Dame's mirror formation put people in position to tackle whoever had the ball. It left the field wide open for the Texas wide receivers, but Notre Dame counted on Ellis and the other defensive backs to handle the added pass defense responsibilities. They preferred to see Texas try to win with an unfamiliar passing game rather than with their favorite wishbone offense.

The extra lineman (#4) would give the Irish more muscle to stop Worster but would do little against Bertelsen's speed. Blitzes (#3) rarely worked against a wishbone because the triple option made it impossible to predict who would end up with the ball.

Here's What Happened!

The wishbone swung into action on the first offensive play of the day. Texas quarterback Phillips spotted an opening in the Irish defense and dashed for 63 yards before the defense caught up with him. The Longhorn drive stalled, but Texas still came away with a field goal for a 3-0 lead. It seemed as though the wishbone offense was still an unsolved puzzle.

For the rest of the game, however, Notre Dame's defense pulled the wheels off the "unstoppable" Texas offense. After that first run by Phillips, Texas managed only 153 more rushing yards in the game. Worster, playing with nagging injuries, found the going tougher in this game than in the 1970 Cotton Bowl. He fought for 42 yards in 16 carries, an average of less than three yards per try. Bertelsen never found anyplace to run, as he picked up a meager five yards total for the day!

In all, Notre Dame stopped wishbone running plays for gains of one yard or less 19 times. On a key fourth down with one yard to go at the Irish 35-yard line, Bertelsen was stopped cold and Notre Dame took over the ball. The flustered Longhorns helped out their opponents with nine fumbles, four by the usually sure-handed Worster.

With their running throttled, Texas took to the air. Although Eddie Phillips passed and ran well enough to win the game's Most Valuable Player Award, Clarence Ellis stopped enough crucial passes to keep Texas out of the end zone. Texas did not score at all in the second half and were held to their lowest point total in three years as they lost 24-11.

Bloodied and beaten, Texas fullback Steve Worster sits dejectedly on the bench.

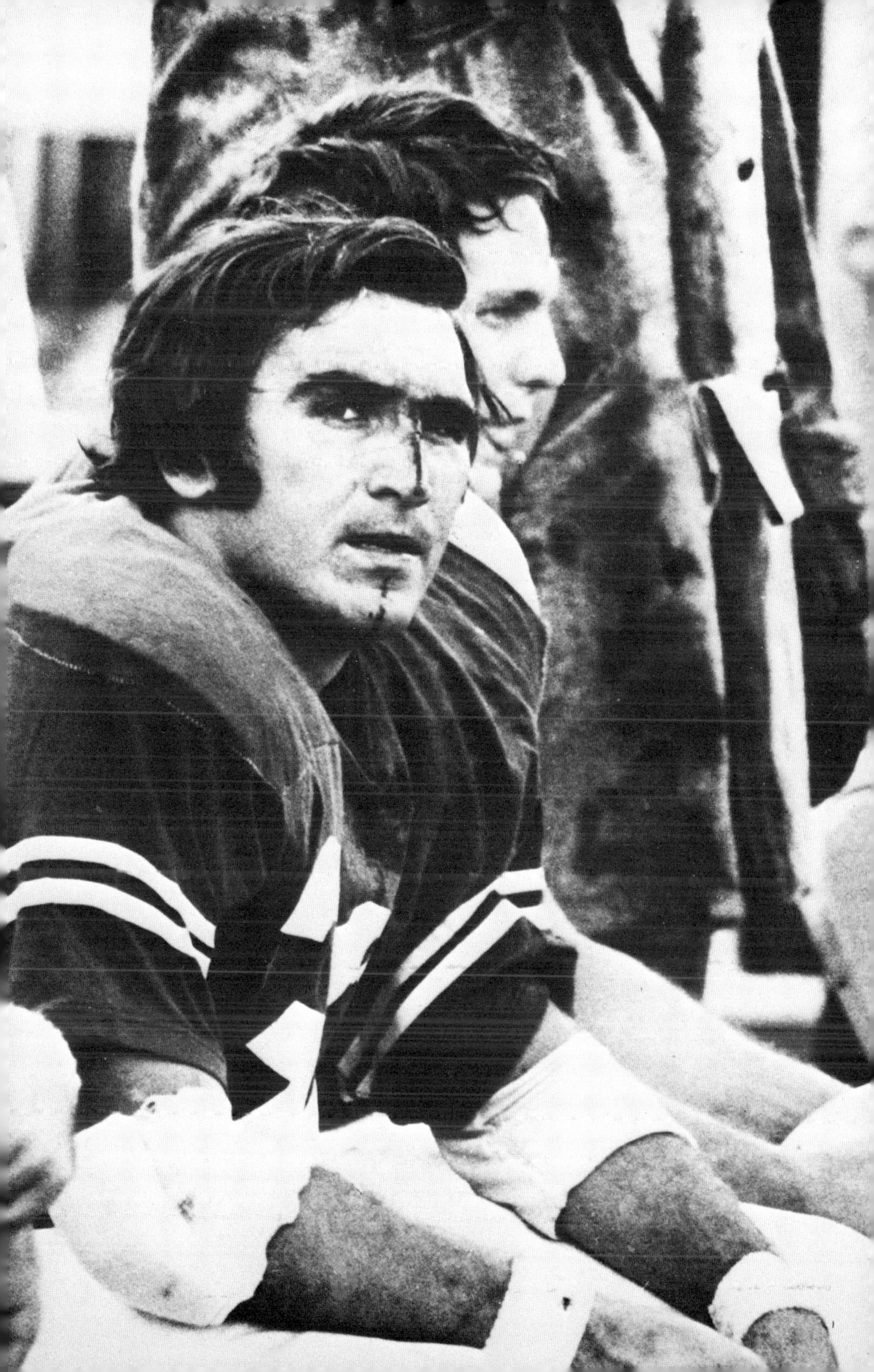

7 Keeping Up With the Joneses
(and Smiths, and Washingtons...)

Michigan State's Clint Jones, Bubba Smith, and Gene Washington are three of college football's brightest stars. How can the underdog UCLA Bruins eclipse them?

You are coaching the UCLA Bruins.

It is your bad luck to have guided your team to the Rose Bowl at a time when Michigan State University has put together its best team in the school's history. The Spartans are so tough that your Bruins are 14½-point underdogs in this 1966 New Year's Day contest, an almost unheard-of margin for this normally competitive bowl game.

You know that it will take some luck, as well as lots of hard work, for your team to keep the score close. Your team's hard work has paid off in a scoreless first period. And now a stroke of luck has come your way. You gained a few yards on the Spartans and then punted deep into their end. Michigan State fumbled the punt, and your team recovered on their six. From there you scored a touchdown to take a surprising 7-0 lead.

When you are as much an underdog as the Bruins are, every decision is crucial. This next kickoff may seem routine, but you still must consider what kind of kick you want to use.

67

Close-Up:
The Michigan State Offense

The Spartan offense is led by three All-American choices, Clint Jones, Gene Washington, and Steve Juday. Jones, at 6 feet, 1 inch, and 208 pounds, is a slashing runner who has gained 787 yards this season. While he doesn't have exceptional speed, moves, or power, he has enough of all three to be a dangerous runner. There is far more speed in the legs of Gene Washington, the Big Ten Conference hurdle champ. This wide receiver often manages to get behind the opponents' defense for a long touchdown.

Steve Juday   Bob Apisa

Despite these two game-breakers, Michigan State has not been a big-play team. Although he has set 12 Spartan passing records, quarterback Steve Juday is not the type to fill the air with passes. A fine runner and a smart play-caller, Juday likes to pick at the defense to snoop out its weaknesses.

These players, plus powerful fullback Bob Apisa, make you wonder why Michigan State hasn't scored a lot of points this year. Perhaps it's because it's more fun to watch the defense at work!

This year's Michigan State defense boasts the 280-pound All-American middle guard Harold Lucas teamed with 270-pound Charles "Bubba" Smith, who has become a legend in his junior year for engulfing both runners and blockers. Elsewhere on the field, 218-pound defensive back George Webster pounces on anything that gets by the defensive line.

Because of this superb defensive unit, the Spartan offense rarely tries anything risky. They prefer to let their defense put them into good field position and then grind away at their opponent until their advantage in size, strength, and talent begins to show.

Harold Lucas   George Webster

Close-Up:
The UCLA Defense

In contrast to Michigan State, you don't have a single All-American on your team. Your starless defense plays well as a team, however. You played at Michigan State in the opening game of the season and lost only 13-3, so your defenders have no reason to fear the Spartan offense. So far today, your defense has played with extra enthusiasm and has held the Spartan offense in check. Looking over at the huge, swift athletes on the Michigan State sideline, though, you're worried about the Spartans' ability to wear down your team with their superior strength. Now as you bring your kicker, Kurt Zimmerman, onto the field, you must assess what kind of kick he should make.

You have three ways to kick the ball.

Kick it high and deep. If Zimmerman kicks the ball deep, with luck the ball will sail into the end zone and be brought out to the 20 with no kick return. More likely, the Spartans will return the kick to somewhere between the 20- and 30-yard lines. This is the safest of your options. Remember that Michigan State has not pulled off many long drives this year, and you're confident they won't do it against your defense this early in the game. There is only a slim chance that the Spartans could score a touchdown on the return.

Kick a low spinner. If your kicker tries a low, spinning bouncer, you may recover again deep in Spartan territory. Here you would be counting on Michigan State's kick returners being shaky after fumbling away the last punt and giving you a touchdown. A spinning kick might get away from a panicky receiver. On the other hand, if a low kick is fielded properly, there is a greater chance for a long return.

Try an onside kick. You may also recover the ball if your kicker tries an onside kick. Some coaches feel it's best to take charge after you've made a big play. If your team kicks the ball 10 yards and then recovers it, the ball goes back to your offense. This would give you the ball in Spartan territory with another good chance for a score.

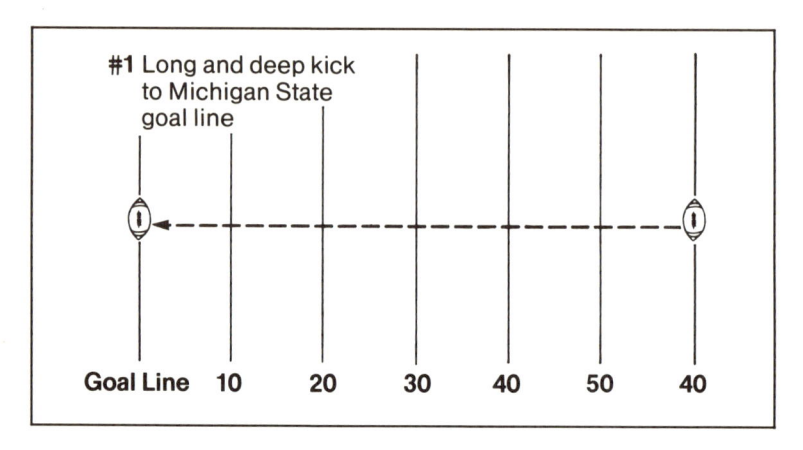

#1 Long and deep kick to Michigan State goal line

Goal Line | 10 | 20 | 30 | 40 | 50 | 40

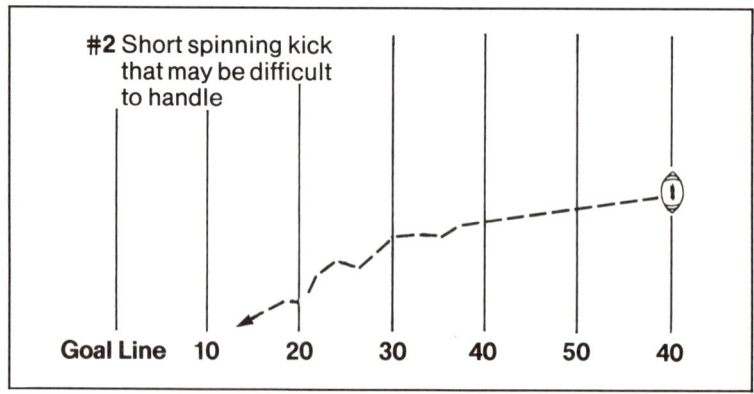

#2 Short spinning kick that may be difficult to handle

Goal Line | 10 | 20 | 30 | 40 | 50 | 40

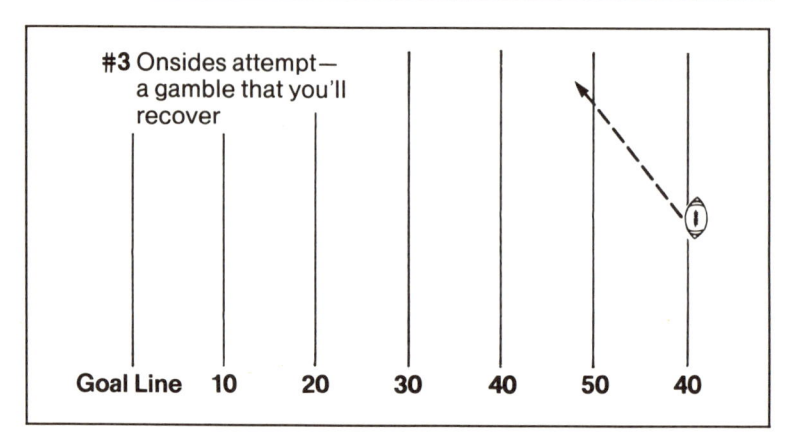

#3 Onsides attempt— a gamble that you'll recover

Goal Line | 10 | 20 | 30 | 40 | 50 | 40

Quarterback Gary Beban now has a full year of college experience. He has been playing well today, both with his running and passing. Given good field position, he might be able to move your Bruins in for another score. Figuring that you may not get another good scoring chance, you may want to take the risk. It _is_ a high-risk play, however, and one that fails more often than not. If Michigan State should recover, you will have given them the field position _they_ need. Experience has taught you that once you lose field position against Michigan State, it's almost impossible to get it back.

What's Your Decision?

> You are the coach.
> You now have an unexpected second-quarter lead.
> **What will you do on the kickoff?**
>
> #1 Kick it high and deep.
> #2 Kick a low spinner.
> #3 Try an onside kick.

Choose the method. Then turn the page to find out which method the UCLA coach chose.

UCLA decided to gamble on #3.

As the heavy underdog, UCLA could afford to play a risky, wide-open game. Since they weren't expected to win anyway, there wasn't any pressure on them to play cautiously to avoid mistakes. UCLA wanted to press the attack while Michigan State was still reeling from the sudden UCLA touchdown. They hoped that an onside kick would catch the wounded Spartans napping.

Here's What Happened!

Bruin kicker Kurt Zimmerman approached the ball as the Spartans waited in their usual kick-return formation. At the last instant, Zimmerman slowed his approach and gave it a soft tap instead of a hard kick. In the mad scramble to recover the ball, UCLA linebacker Dallas Grider was the first to arrive. He fell on the ball at the Spartan 42, and the UCLA offense raced back onto the field. In only four plays, they stormed through the stunned Spartan defense to the one-yard line. From there, Beban again carried the ball into the end zone for a 14-0 lead.

The score stayed that way until the Spartans began overpowering their opponent in the fourth quarter. They scored two touchdowns in the final minutes but failed on both two-point conversion tries, leaving the Bruins with a 14-12 win. Despite only 212 yards of total offense, the Bruins pulled off their huge upset because of the successful onside kick.

UCLA quarterback Gary Beban is hauled down after a 27-yard gain.

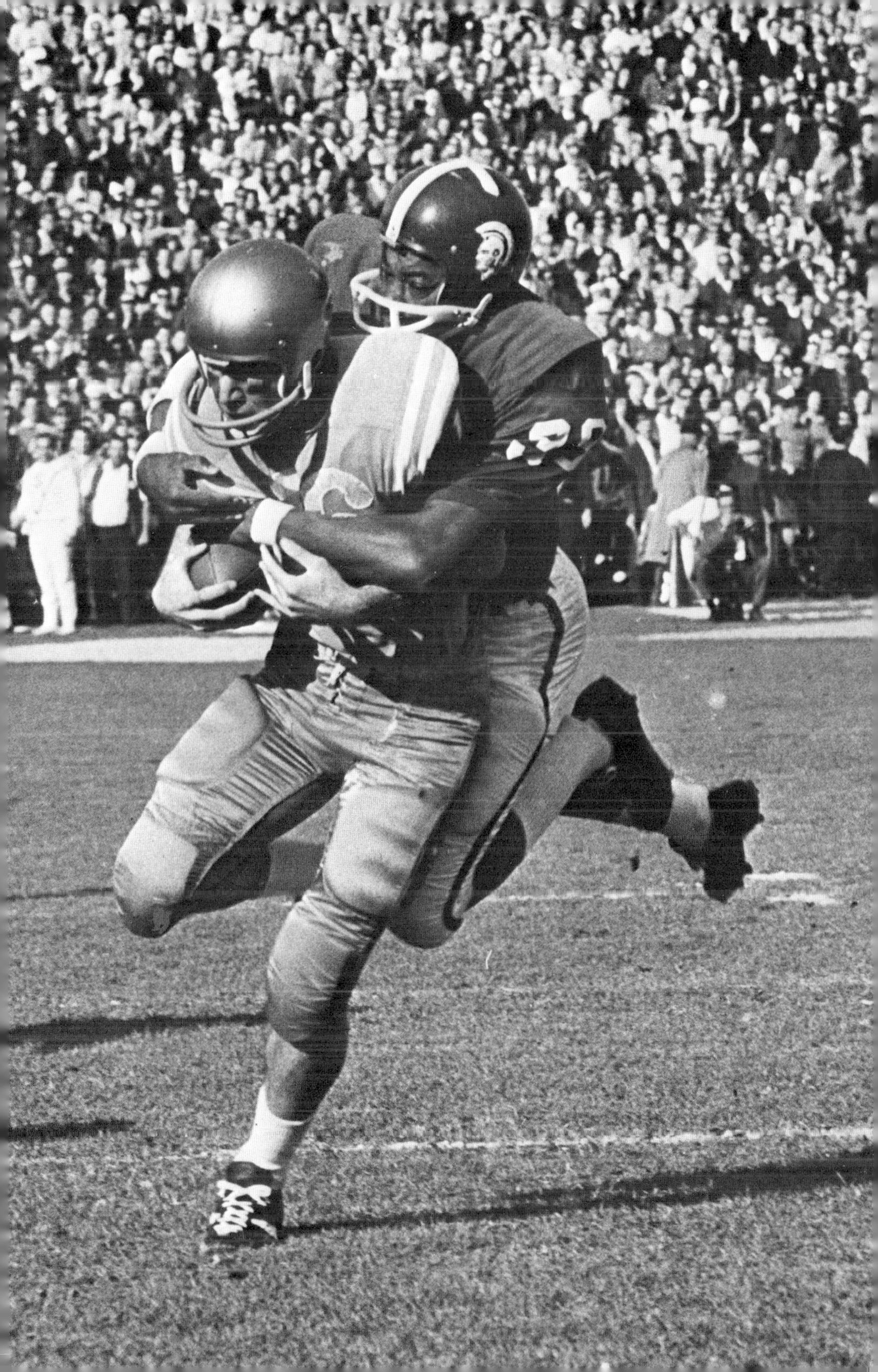

8 Rising Tide

The powerful Alabama defense throws Notre Dame quarterback Tom Clements back for no gain.

You are coaching the Notre Dame Fighting Irish.

Have you ever felt that the ground around you is going to collapse with the very next step you take? As the Notre Dame offense huddles on the field during the Sugar Bowl, their backers sense that this 1973 season is going to end in a sickening thud. The University of Alabama used a trick pass to quarterback Richard Todd to take a 23-21 lead late in the fourth quarter. Then, after you went ahead 24-23 and forced Alabama to punt, the big blow came. Alabama's punt sailed 69 yards and stopped just short of your goal line!

The Crimson Tide defense, charging like a lion after a cornered zebra, has stopped you on two straight carries. Now, with about two minutes left to go, you face a third and eight on your own two-yard line. If you fail to make the first down, you will have trouble even getting your punt out of range of a winning Alabama field goal. Do you have a play ready for this situation?

Close-Up: Alabama

You'll need to consider both Alabama's offense <u>and</u> defense. Undefeated Alabama is rated the top team in the country, which is not unusual for them. As always, their defense is lean, tough, and quick. Their hard hitting has made it tough for your backs to hang onto the football. If they force a fumble now or tackle your runner in the end zone, the game is lost. One player capable of doing just that is linebacker Woodrow Lowe. Alabama coaches rate Lowe as a better defender than ex-Alabama star Lee Roy Jordan, who now stars in the pros. Although Mike Washington has impressed pro scouts, neither he nor the other Tide backs have come up with any interceptions in this game.

If you are forced to punt, Alabama has the strength to drive for a winning score. This is the team that set an NCAA record with 748 rushing yards in a 77-6 win over Virginia Polytechnic. With so little time left in the game, though, Alabama will have to try a pass or two for some quick gains. Quarterbacks Gary Rutledge and Richard Todd have led their team to an incredible average of 24.8 yards per completion!

If Alabama gets reasonably close to the Irish goal, Bill Davis is capable of kicking the winning field goal for them. He has made one from 39 yards away earlier in this game but has also missed an extra point.

Surrounded by Irish defenders, Alabama quarterback Gary Rutledge pitches out to one of his running backs in second-quarter action.

Close-Up: The Notre Dame Offense

The Irish have always been known as a power team with plenty of beef in their offensive line. This year, your team still has large blockers, but there are no All-American candidates among them. Fullback Wayne Bullock, at 6 feet and 220 pounds, fits his name perfectly. Bullock is used often, works hard, and does nothing fancy. He is almost always good for a short gain, and he rarely fumbles.

Notre Dame has also pumped some speed into the backfield this season. Eric Penick weighs 215 pounds but can run 100 yards in 9.5 seconds. Although he is learning to protect the ball, he has fumbled frequently in his career. Art Best is another good runner with size (200 pounds), speed (9.7 seconds in the 100), and better hands than Penick's. Neither speedster has been able to get away from the quick Alabama defense in this game, however.

Quarterback Tom Clements has been your most effective runner today. While not as flashy as recent Notre Dame quarterbacks such as Joe Theismann, Clements is a leader. He runs well, throws accurately, and directs the offense with poise.

Eric Penick    Art Best

Tom Clements    Dave Casper

The best of Clements' receivers is tight end Dave Casper. At 230 pounds, Casper can't outsprint many defenders, but he can hold onto almost any ball thrown his way. Receivers Pete Demmerle and Robin Weber have not been used as often. Although you have confidence in your passing game, a forward pass in this situation is a big risk. Even if you avoid an interception, an incomplete pass will stop the clock and give Alabama more time to score.

You know that you have the nation's second-best defense to protect your lead. You don't want to give away the game on a turnover, you can't afford an incomplete pass, and yet you don't want to punt.

What's Your Decision?

You are the coach.
With only two minutes left, you lead by one point and face a third down and eight on your own two-yard line. This play may decide the game.
What will you call?

#1 Try a short pass to Casper.
#2 Send Bullock straight ahead.
#3 Send Best around end.
#4 Try a long pass to a wide receiver.
#5 Let Clements run with the ball.

Choose the play. Then turn the page to find out which play the Notre Dame coach chose.

Notre Dame decided to try #4.

Part of Coach Ara Parseghian's reasoning went back to a game played many years before. At the end of a brilliantly played game between his top-ranked team and the number-two Spartans of Michigan State, Parseghian chose to run out the clock rather than try to break a 10-10 tie. People have criticized him ever since for that unheroic move. This time, Ara chose the boldest move possible, a long pass.

Long passes are not often completed, and an incomplete pass would stop the clock for Alabama. But Notre Dame had confidence in the accurate arm of Clements. They also knew that Alabama would not be expecting that type of play. Most teams play very cautiously that close to their own goal line, especially with a lead in the last minutes of the game. Notre Dame, though, decided that the game had to be won on the next play in order to stop the surging Crimson Tide.

Here's What Happened!

Clements faked a handoff to his running backs and then drifted back into his end zone. The Alabama backs reacted quickly to the surprise play and had most of the Irish receivers well covered. Robin Weber, however, was running a deep sideline pattern where the Crimson Tide least expected him. Clements needed a perfect pass to keep from leading Weber out of bounds. At first Parseghian thought Clements had overthrown his receiver, but Weber came down with the ball before going out of bounds in front of the Alabama bench. The play moved the ball all the way out to the 38-yard line and gave Notre Dame the first down they needed to protect their lead.

Alabama coach Bear Bryant said that after his team's punt pinned the Irish inside their own one-yard line, he would have bet his life that his team was going to win the game. But thanks to a bold gamble and a poised effort by quarterback Tom Clements, Notre Dame jumped past Alabama into the number-one ranking.

9 Night of the Defense

Though defenses could be expected to dominate this Orange Bowl, here Michigan's Jim Smith manages to get past the Sooner defensive unit in the first quarter. Can your offense slip by their equally tough defense as well?

You are coaching the University of Oklahoma Sooners.

There have been complaints that the hard and uneven Orange Bowl turf has made this the most dangerous field for football. But the special hazard on this New Year's night, 1976, is not the turf but the defensive units of both the Sooners and the University of Michigan Wolverines.

The offensive units of each team must feel like they are squeezed in a vise. Both teams field hard-nosed tacklers who are greatly responsible for the fact that each of the schools has lost only three regular-season games in the last five years. But neither the Sooners' deadly wishbone offense nor Michigan's "power-I" running attack has gone anywhere in the first quarter of this game.

In the second quarter you resorted to a rare long pass from your own 21-yard line. Michigan defender Dwight Hicks had such tight coverage on your Tinker Owens that he had the receiver all but gift wrapped. But Owens still came down with the ball. This first big play of the game covered 40 yards to the Wolverine 39. There aren't likely to be many such plays tonight. How will you take advantage of it?

85

Close-Up:
The Michigan Defense

The Wolverines, ranked number five, are smaller than your Sooners, but they make up for their size with ferocious play. Despite their brilliant record, this is the first time that the Wolverine seniors have been invited to a bowl game, and they are determined to make it a good one. Their defensive linemen have been charging in at different angles, and their linebackers have roared in on all kinds of blitzes. This has confused your blockers and has you groping for plays that will work. Michigan's hot-pursuing, gang-tackling team actually held you without a first down on your first two offensive series.

That type of experience may be new to your Sooners, but it's just a typical day's work for the Wolverines. Even though they lost their only game of the year to the Ohio State Buckeyes, they could take pride in what they did to Buckeye back Archie Griffin. A two-time Heisman Trophy winner, Griffin was held to 46 yards in 19 carries, the first time in 31 regular-season games that he didn't make 100 yards or more.

Leaders of the Michigan defense are Don Dufek and Dan Jilek. Dufek plays a combination of free safety and linebacker and acts as the team's designated tackler. Jilek, an end, has been outstanding so far tonight.

Close-Up:
The Oklahoma Offense

Your version of the wishbone attack is operated by quarterback Steve Davis, a three-year starter. Davis' experience at reading the reactions of the defense make the triple option successful. In the triple option, Davis can make the split second pitchout to make his running attack go, he can pass to a receiver downfield, or he can run the ball himself. When it comes to precise exchanges such as those needed on pitchouts, though, Davis and the Sooners are far from perfect. Oklahoma has dropped an incredible 58 fumbles this season, including 13 in a single game!

As with most wishbone teams, Oklahoma uses the pass only as a surprise weapon. Most of Davis' passes go to little Tinker Owens, a 170-pound version of his big brother Steve, a hard-running Heisman Trophy winner from a few years ago. Right now Owens is out of the game catching his breath after that long pass.

Steve Davis   Tinker Owens

His replacement, Billy Brooks, is faster than Owens but hasn't been used much as a receiver. Brooks has shown skill, though, at running reverses.

Your backfield could do well in a sprint relay race. You have two raw speedsters, Horace Ivory and young Elvis Peacock. But the best of the lot is 5-foot, 9-inch 185-pound wriggler Joe Washington. With eel-like moves and an uncanny sense for escaping tacklers, Joe is fun to watch, especially if he gets into the open field. All three are best at running to the outside, but Michigan rarely allows a runner much progress on that route.

Michigan's Gordon Bell gets a Selmon sandwich when Oklahoma's brother act of Dewey (91) and Lee Roy combine to hit him high and low.

When you need inside power, you turn to Jim Littrell or Jim Culbreath. Neither is a dominating runner, though.

Because of the strength of your defense, you can afford to gamble on offense when you are in Michigan territory. Your Sooners have survived those 58 fumbles this season because no one could move the ball against the Selmon brothers, Lee Roy and Dewey, and linebacker Jimbo Elrod.

What's Your Decision?

You are the coach.
Number-one-rated Ohio State has just lost the Rose Bowl, meaning the national title is yours if you win this Orange Bowl. The game is scoreless in the second quarter.
How will you take advantage of your first big offensive gain against this rugged Wolverine defense?

#1 Come back with another long pass.

#2 Have Brooks come around from his wide receiver spot to run a reverse.

#3 Fake a pass and send Washington on a delayed run up the middle.

#4 Have Davis direct your usual triple option.

Choose the play. Then turn the page to find out what the Oklahoma coach chose.

Oklahoma decided on #2.

This is one of those trick plays that must be used carefully and rarely more than once a game. Since it takes a long time to get a play like this moving, it can be easily stopped for a 10- or 15-yard loss if the defense is ready. Oklahoma thought that this would be a good time to try the play because Brooks, their best reverse runner, happened to be in the game for the winded Owens.

The Sooners went along with the theory of following up one surprise big play with another surprise big play while the defense is still rattled. Since they did not pass that well (#1), especially without Owens in the lineup, the reverse was the best big-play gamble left to choose from.

OKLAHOMA REVERSE

The Sooners fake a run up the middle (1); Davis keeps the ball and then pitches back (2) to Brooks (3) who is coming the opposite way from his split end spot. Brooks continues around the opposite end (4).

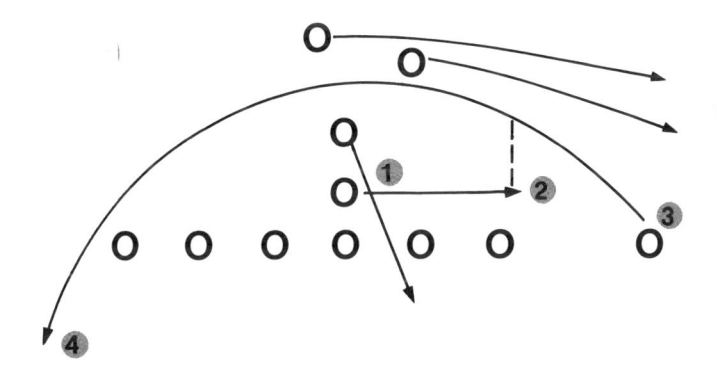

O Oklahoma Offense

Here's What Happened!

Quarterback Davis ran to the left side behind good blocking from his line. It looked like the usual Sooner wishbone option. Brooks, who had lined up on the left side, swung around behind Davis and took the pitch from his quarterback on the run.

No sooner had Brooks caught the ball than he found himself face to face with Michigan end Jilek.

The Oklahoma runner screeched to a halt, faked out the Wolverine, and dashed into the clear. Only one other defender had a chance to stop him, as the rest had all rushed off after Davis. Brooks slipped past the last defender at the 20 and raced in for the score, untouched. Oklahoma's big play led to a 14-6 win, helping them claim the nation's number-one spot.

The Big Play: Billy Brooks side-steps Michigan's Dan Jilek on the reverse that gave Oklahoma their first score.

10 "How 'Bout Them Dawgs!"

In this Sugar Bowl, Pitt showed it could do what few other teams had ever done—contain the great Georgia runner Herschel Walker.

You are coaching
the University of Georgia Bulldogs.

Your Georgia team has been playing so well that the most common conversation starter in the state is "How 'bout them Dawgs!" Your Bulldogs finished first in the polls last year and are rated number two this season. Right now they are holding on to a slim lead over a tough University of Pittsburgh team in this 1982 Sugar Bowl game.

It hasn't been easy. The Pitt Panthers have outplayed your team throughout the game. Their top-ranked defense has held your star runner, Herschel Walker, to 84 yards in 25 carries, and your offense to 224 total yards. But your amazing "Dawgs" have scrapped their way to a 20-17 lead. All you need is one more defensive play and this Sugar Bowl win is yours.

Pittsburgh faces a fourth down and 5 on your 33-yard line with only 42 seconds left to play. Their quarterback, Dan Marino, has enjoyed a good passing game against you. What defense do you order to stop Pitt?

Close-Up:
The Pittsburgh Offense

The one player most responsible for Pittsburgh's success is quarterback Dan Marino. His coach claims that Marino is better than pro stars Ken Stabler and Joe Namath were at the same age. Marino stays calm in frenzied moments and has a rare talent for detecting what defenses are up to. Given time to throw, Marino can strike quickly with accurate passes. He has been well protected this game and has completed 25 of 40 passes for 228 yards and two touchdowns. Although not fond of running the ball, Dan kept this drive going earlier when he picked up the needed yards on a fourth-down quarterback draw.

There is no shortage of pass targets for Marino. His favorite receiver this season has been Julius Dawkins. The two have teamed up again in this game for 8 completions, 64 yards, and 1 touchdown. Tight end John Brown has been open on short pass routes so far, with five catches for 29 yards, including a touchdown. Flanker Dwight Collins and backs Wayne DiBartola and Bryan Thomas give Pittsburgh five sure-handed receivers on the field at one time.

Thomas has provided most of the legwork for a running game that has totaled 206 yards. His 129 yards in 25 carries averages out to about the distance Pittsburgh needs for this first down.

John Brown

Dan Marino

Close-Up:
The Georgia Defense

With Herschel Walker soaking up all the attention, Georgia's defense is a mystery to most people. But they have a good unit led by All-Conference lineman Jimmy Payne. Payne has been barreling in on quarterbacks all year and leads the team with 12 sacks. Eddie Weaver, a 270-pound tackle, leads the charge against running plays.

The Bulldog defense is quite young for such a highly ranked team. Eight of the eleven starters are

Jimmy Payne

Eddie Weaver

Dale Williams

Ronnie Harris

underclassmen. The least experienced position for you is at defensive back, where you can least afford it against someone like Marino. Dale Williams is the only senior in the backfield.

You do have a big-play man, speedy Ronnie Harris, at cornerback. Ronnie has intercepted four passes this season. Earlier in the game he wiped out an almost certain Pittsburgh score with an interception at the goal line.

In this situation, your defense also has time on its side. With only 42 seconds left, Pittsburgh will have to hurry to score. Even if they get a first down, they may not have time to move in for a winning tally.

What's Your Decision?

You are the coach.
Pittsburgh is going into their huddle now, making plans to salvage this game. **What strategy will your young defense carry out?**

#1 Go into a "prevent" defense. In other words, give them the short pass, but guard against anything deep.

#2 Guard against the short pass.

#3 Have your linebackers come up to play against a run.

#4 Send all the linebackers in on a blitz.

Choose the strategy. Then turn the page to see which strategy the Georgia coach chose.

Georgia sent out instructions to go with #4.

The Bulldogs had not been getting a good pass rush against Marino, which helped account for Pittsburgh's great passing success in this game. Georgia hoped that a blitz would catch the Panthers off guard and disrupt the play. A blitz is also a good defense against running plays, so this would work against either a pass or a running play. Of course, there was a danger that Pittsburgh's blockers would hold off all of the pass rushers, leaving you with only three inexperienced players to cover the entire field. But Georgia felt they had to take charge of the game with an aggressive defense rather than depend on their usual defensive strategy (#1, #2). With so little time left, and five yards to go for a first down, the Bulldogs were not afraid of a run (#3).

Here's What Happened!

Pittsburgh chose a play called 69-X, which sent five players out to run pass patterns. The two backs were to cross over the middle, and the three others were to go straight downfield. The Panthers hoped to clear out some room for Thomas to make the catch and run for some extra yards. When the Bulldogs fired into the backfield from all sides, though, that plan had to be scrapped. Thomas had to stay in the backfield to block one of the blitzers.

WHAT GEORGIA'S DEFENSE FACED (PLAY 69-X):
Pittsburgh planned to send three receivers (3,4,5) downfield, with the backs (1,2) running shorter crossing routes over the middle.

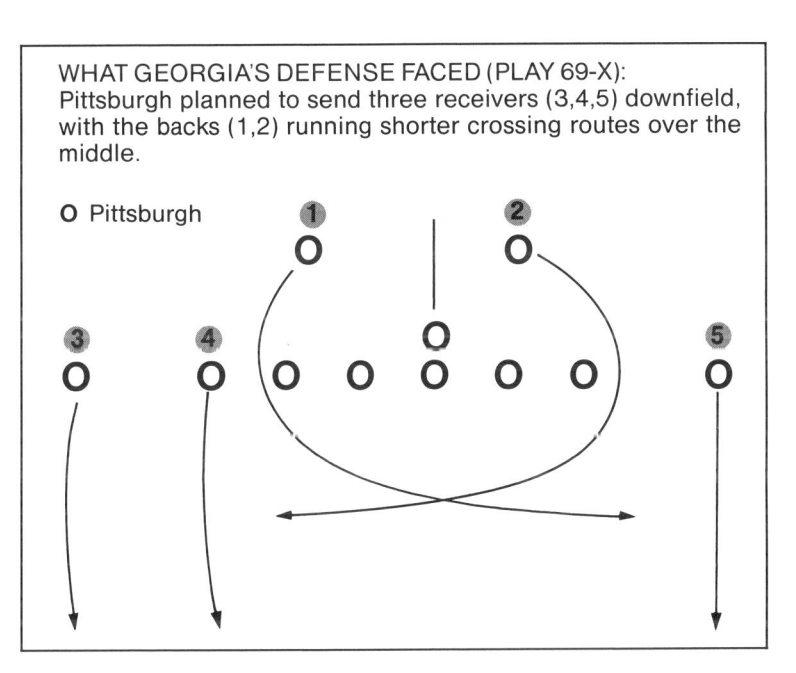

O Pittsburgh

Georgia's blitz forced the running backs (1,2) to stay in to block but left three receivers (3,4,5) with only one man each to beat.

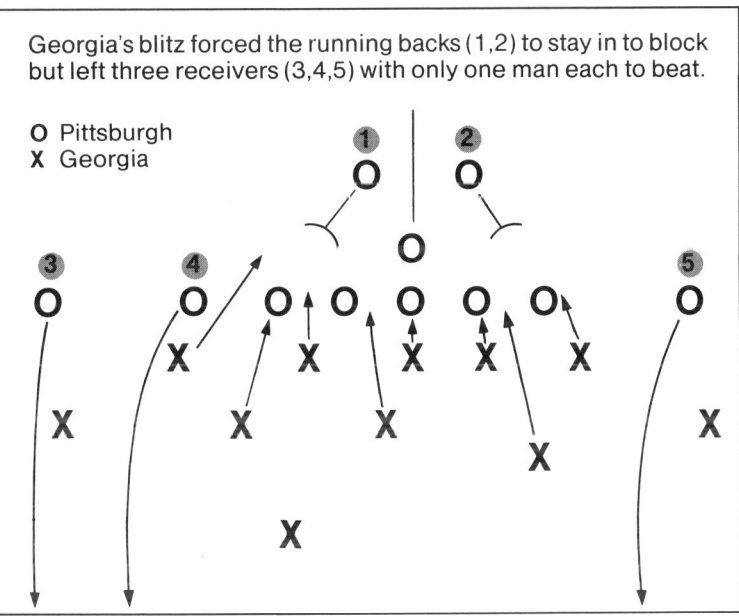

O Pittsburgh
X Georgia

101

Pittsburgh quarterback Marino had quickly recognized that a blitz was coming. Knowing that there were few Bulldogs left to defend against the pass, he looked far downfield for a receiver. John Brown was just racing past a Georgia safety when Marino hurled his pass. The timing was perfect as the sprinting Brown latched onto the ball in the end zone. The 33-yard touchdown gave Pittsburgh a thrilling 24-20 win. Georgia's strategy had backfired, and the Bulldogs were left to wonder what would have happened if they had chosen instead to play it safe.

Pitt's John Brown clutches Dan Marino's 33-yard pass in the end zone to give the Panthers a come-from-behind Sugar Bowl win.

ACKNOWLEDGMENTS

Photo credits: pp. 66, 68, 69, Michigan State University; p. 12, Ohio State University; pp. 20, 48, 49, Penn State University; p. 24, Stanford University; p. 4, Phil Steinberg; p. 7, Tournament of Roses Association; pp. 19, 40, 41, University of Alabama; p. 98, University of Georgia; p. 47, University of Kansas; p. 27, University of Michigan; pp. 60, 80, University of Notre Dame; p. 87, University of Oklahoma; p. 97, University of Pittsburgh; p. 9, University of Southern California; pp. 38, 56, University of Texas; pp. 10, 15, 23, 28, 35, 36, 55, 76, 79, 84, 92-93, 94, 103, United Press International; pp. 16, 43, 44, 50, 65, 75, 88, Wide World Photos, Inc.

The play diagrams appear through the courtesy of: p. 58, University of Texas; p. 91, University of Oklahoma.

Cover photograph: Manny Millan/SPORTS ILLUSTRATED

Also by Nate Aaseng

COLLEGE BASKETBALL: YOU ARE THE COACH
10 exciting NCAA final four games

BASEBALL: YOU ARE THE MANAGER
10 exciting championship games

BASKETBALL: YOU ARE THE COACH
10 exciting NBA play-off games

FOOTBALL: YOU ARE THE COACH
10 exciting NFL play-off games

HOCKEY: YOU ARE THE COACH
10 exciting NHL play-off
and international games

Lerner Publications Company
241 First Avenue North, Minneapolis, MN 55401

MILLCREEK — WEST UNITY SCHOOLS
WEST UNITY OHIO